W9-CFJ-414

CHILDREN'S AUTHORS

CYNTHIA KADOHATA

Jill C. Wheeler

ABDO Publishing Company

visit us at
www.abdopublishing.com

Published by ABDO Publishing Company, PO Box 398166, Minneapolis, Minnesota 55439.
Copyright © 2013 by Abdo Consulting Group, Inc. International copyrights reserved in all
countries. No part of this book may be reproduced in any form without written permission from the
publisher. The Checkerboard Library™ is a trademark and logo of ABDO Publishing Company.

Printed in the United States of America, North Mankato, Minnesota.
102012
012013

 PRINTED ON RECYCLED PAPER

Cover Photo: AP Images
Interior Photos: AP Images p. 5; Corbis pp. 13, 17; George Miyamoto pp. 19, 21;
    Glow Images pp. 9, 11; @Julia Kuskin p. 15; Michael Frost p. 18; Shane Rebenschied p. 20

Special thanks to Cynthia Kadohata for the images on pp. 7, 10

Series Coordinator: Megan M. Gunderson
Editors: Megan M. Gunderson, BreAnn Rumsch
Art Direction: Neil Klinepier

Cataloging-in-Publication Data

Wheeler, Jill C., 1964-
 Cynthia Kadohata / Jill C. Wheeler.
   p. cm. -- (Children's authors)
Includes bibliographical references and index.
ISBN 978-1-61783-575-9
1. Kadohata, Cynthia, 1956- --Juvenile literature. 2. Authors, Japanese-American--Biography--
Juvenile literature. 3. Women authors, Japanese-American--Biography--Juvenile literature. 4.
Children's stories--Authorship--Juvenile literature. I. Title.
813/.6--dc23
[B]

2012946382

CONTENTS

Seeking Inspiration

Cynthia Kadohata has always been a wanderer. Growing up, she moved from state to state. As an adult, she continued traveling to find inspiration. Her experiences helped her become a creative and successful writer.

Kadohata draws her stories from her memory as well as from her imagination. She has written books and short stories for both children and adults. Reviewers have loved her work. Kadohata's most famous book is *Kira-Kira*. This novel earned her the **Newbery Medal** in 2005.

Often, people ask Kadohata what advice she would give to new writers. She tells them to think about their own lives when looking for things to write about. She believes writers should remember the sad things as well as the happy things. Together, these experiences make people who they are.

Kadohata *is an unusual name, even in Japan.*

Growing Up a Southern Girl

Cynthia Kadohata was born on July 2, 1956, in Chicago, Illinois. She grew up with an older sister and a younger brother. Both of Cynthia's parents were of Japanese descent. But, they had been born in the United States. Cynthia's father worked in agriculture. Her mother took care of the children and later earned a law degree.

When Cynthia was very young, her family left Illinois for Georgia. There, her father found a job at a chicken hatchery. The work was difficult and unpleasant. It also was done almost entirely by people of Japanese heritage. Cynthia and her family spent much of their time with this tight-knit community.

Then in 1958, the family moved to Arkansas. There, Cynthia's father continued working in the poultry industry.

When Cynthia was nine, her parents divorced. She and her mother, sister, and brother moved to Michigan for a while. Then they returned to Chicago. Her father stayed in Arkansas, but Cynthia still saw him regularly.

Cynthia (right) with her brother and sister in Arkansas in 1961

While living in the South, Cynthia had picked up a heavy Southern accent. But in Chicago, a teacher threatened to put her in speech therapy if she didn't lose it. No one there could understand the way she spoke!

FINDING AN EDUCATION

Cynthia's mother had been born in Southern California. She returned there with her children when Cynthia was 15. In Los Angeles, Cynthia attended Hollywood High School. But during her senior year, Cynthia dropped out of school.

At this time, Cynthia was painfully shy. Even the thought of talking with a store clerk made her nervous. Still, she took on a series of jobs. She became a department store clerk. And, she worked as a hamburger server in a fast-food restaurant.

When she was young, Cynthia had usually had a book in her hands. After leaving school, she rediscovered her love of reading. She spent hours at the local library.

Cynthia also tried writing. At 17, she wrote an odd short story about a planet **inhabited** only by one-legged ducks. Cynthia sent it to the *Atlantic Monthly* in the hopes of getting it published. But the magazine rejected her story. This was her first of many rejections.

At 18, Cynthia began studying at Los Angeles City College. There, several teachers encouraged and inspired her to pursue writing. And, Cynthia worked on newspapers with her friends. She stayed up late writing and editing. Later, Cynthia transferred to the University of Southern California (USC). She graduated with a degree in **journalism** in 1977.

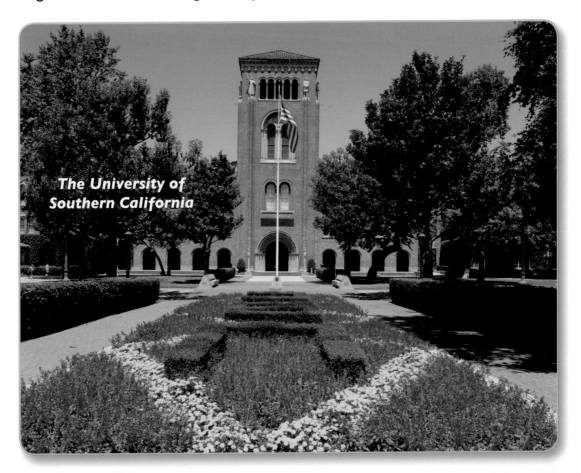

The University of Southern California

THE ROAD TO WRITING

Kadohata's life changed forever when she was just 21. One day while she was walking in Los Angeles, a car ran over the curb and hit her. The accident broke her collarbone and severely injured her right arm. Kadohata's collarbone healed, but her arm would never be the same.

Badly shaken, Kadohata moved to Boston, Massachusetts, where her sister lived. There, she held a series of temporary office jobs. Kadohata spent her spare time browsing in the city's many bookstores. This gave Kadohata the idea of writing fiction.

Kadohata poured her energy into writing short stories. She challenged herself to write one a month. She began

Kadohata received 25 rejection letters from the New Yorker before they accepted one of her stories.

Columbia University

sending them off to magazines, including the *Atlantic Monthly* and the *New Yorker*. She wrote 20 to 40 stories and received rejection letters for all of them. Yet some of the letters encouraged her to keep writing, so she kept going.

Eventually, Kadohata's hard work paid off. In 1986, the *New Yorker* accepted one of her stories! She followed that success with published stories in other magazines.

Later that year, she entered a graduate fiction-writing program at the University of Pittsburgh in Pennsylvania. But soon, she transferred to the writing program at New York's Columbia University. Kadohata felt the move would help her writing. And, it would take her to New York City!

PUBLISHED!

At Columbia, Kadohata took classes and kept writing. Soon, **literary agent** Andrew Wylie contacted her. Wylie had read her work in the *New Yorker* and wanted to see more.

The two began building a novel from Kadohata's short stories. The novel mirrors Kadohata's childhood in many ways. It tells the story of a young Japanese-American girl and her family. They travel around America after **World War II** looking for work.

In spring 1988, Wylie sold Kadohata's book *The Floating World* to a publisher. It came out the following year and was well received. Suddenly, Kadohata was a new Asian voice in American literature. In 1991, Kadohata received a $30,000 **Whiting Writers' Award**.

In 1992, Kadohata got married. The same year, she published *In the Heart of the Valley of Love*. The book is a fantasy novel about Los Angeles set in the year 2052. It received mixed reviews, but Kadohata kept writing. Then in

Kadohata had heard of Wylie (above). She thought he was a good agent but a little scary! Yet when they met, Kadohata realized Wylie was smart and kind.

1995, Kadohata published another fantasy novel. *The Glass Mountains* received almost no attention at all.

Next, Kadohata won a $20,000 screenwriting **fellowship**. She tried to write **screenplays**, but she had little success. So, she found herself working as a secretary at a food-processing plant. By the late 1990s, few readers were thinking about her.

A New Challenge

By 2000, Kadohata was divorced and still struggling with her writing. But her career would take a new turn thanks to her former University of Pittsburgh roommate.

Caitlyn Dlouhy was a good friend as well as a children's book editor. She had long encouraged Kadohata to try writing for children. One day, Dlouhy sent her a box of children's books. Kadohata couldn't help but read them! Her other novels had been for adults. But they had featured young main characters. So, she decided to give children's writing a try.

Kadohata gave Dlouhy a list of ideas for possible books. Together, they chose a story that begins much like Kadohata's own life. The story is about a Japanese-American girl named Katie whose family moves from the Midwest to Georgia. Katie helps her family when they find out her sister has **cancer**.

As Kadohata wrote, Dlouhy commented on her work. The partnership was not always easy. But when Dlouhy suggested big changes, she sent Kadohata chocolates to soften the pain!

Kadohata titled the finished book *Kira-Kira*. The book received many good reviews. In 2005, a phone call woke Kadohata at 4:26 AM. The caller told her *Kira-Kira* had won the **Newbery Medal**. Kadohata was thrilled!

Kira-Kira *means "glittering" in Japanese.*

From Memories to Stories

After *Kira-Kira*'s success, Kadohata kept writing for young readers. In 2006, *Weedflower* was published. It tells the story of a young Japanese-American girl named Sumiko.

Sumiko's story begins just before the 1941 bombing of Pearl Harbor, in Hawaii, by Japan. As the United States joins **World War II**, Sumiko and her family must abandon their flower farm in California. They and other Japanese-Americans are sent to an internment camp in the Arizona desert. There, Sumiko makes friends with a young Native American boy.

Internment camps were created to hold certain people based on their **ethnic** backgrounds. The US government believed holding these people would prevent them from spying or being disloyal.

Kadohata had never experienced life in an internment camp. But her father had been sent to the Colorado River Relocation Camp, or Poston. It was on the Colorado River Indian Reservation. Kadohata felt it was important to share this story with modern readers.

During World War II, Japanese Americans were relocated from the West Coast. They were housed in camps in remote areas of the country.

Kadohata's next novel appeared in 2007. *Cracker! The Best Dog in Vietnam* is about a military dog in Vietnam. To write the book, Kadohata had to research military dogs. She learned how they were trained and used to sniff out bombs and traps. She also learned that these dogs were responsible for saving about 10,000 lives during the **Vietnam War**.

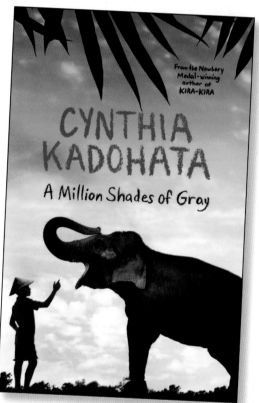

Cracker! received many awards. It was named one of the Bank Street Best Books of the Year. And, it earned a Parents' Choice Award.

Kadohata followed *Cracker!* with a book for older readers called *Outside Beauty*. It is about four stepsisters who split up after their mother has a car accident. They must then find their way back to each other. The book was released in 2008.

Kadohata enjoyed doing research for **A Million Shades of Gray!**

Reviewers praised Kadohata for her characters and their relationships.

In 2010, Kadohata returned to Vietnam as the setting of her next novel. *A Million Shades of Gray* is the story of a Vietnamese boy named Y'Tin who learns to train elephants. He must use this knowledge to save himself after his village is attacked.

An Author's Life

Today, Kadohata lives in Southern California with her son, Sammy. She adopted him from Kazakhstan in 2004. She and Sammy share their home with their pet Doberman, Shika Kojika. Their dog's name means "deer, little deer" in Japanese.

Kadohata remains a frequent traveler. Over the years, she has used travel to help her gain inspiration for her stories. She has also looked to music or even a favorite perfume to spark ideas for new writing projects.

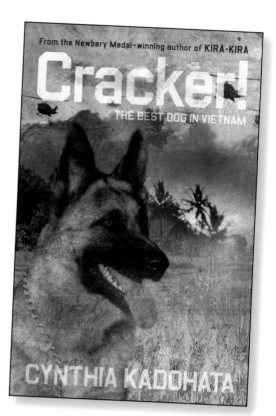

Kadohata's love of dogs shows in Cracker! The book is narrated by a German shepherd.

In addition to dogs and travel, Kadohata loves tacos! This is just like her character Katie in *Kira-Kira*. Kadohata shares similarities with her characters. In fact, she admits she sometimes mixes up things that really happened to her and things that happened to her characters. Once she has written something, it is as if she has experienced it.

Today, Kadohata continues to look for inspiration. She tries to produce a new book every year. With any luck, her fans will not have to wait long for the next one.

Kadohata likes to write about both the past and the future.

GLOSSARY

cancer - any of a group of often deadly diseases marked by harmful changes in the normal growth of cells. Cancer can spread and destroy healthy tissues and organs.

ethnic - of or relating to groups of people organized by race, nationality, religion, or culture.

fellowship - money or a position given to someone to continue their work or studies.

inhabit - to live in or occupy a place.

journalism - the collecting and editing of news to be presented through various media. These include newspapers, magazines, television, and radio. A person who does this is called a journalist.

literary agent - a person who helps an author sell his or her work.

Newbery Medal - an annual award given by the American Library Association. It honors the author of the best American children's book published in the previous year.

screenplay - the written form of a story prepared for a movie.

Vietnam War - from 1957 to 1975. A long, failed attempt by the United States to stop North Vietnam from taking over South Vietnam.

Whiting Writers' Award - an award given annually by the Mrs. Giles Whiting Foundation to ten writers. It honors upcoming writers of fiction, nonfiction, poetry, and plays.

World War II - from 1939 to 1945, fought in Europe, Asia, and Africa. Great Britain, France, the United States, the Soviet Union, and their allies were on one side. Germany, Italy, Japan, and their allies were on the other side.

WEB SITES

To learn more about Cynthia Kadohata, visit ABDO Publishing Company online. Web sites about Cynthia Kadohata are featured on our Book Links page. These links are routinely monitored and updated to provide the most current information available.
www.abdopublishing.com

INDEX

3 1491 01128 4092

Niles
Public Library District
NOV 0 1 2013

Niles, Illinois 60714